What Children Know about Angels

Dandi Daley Mackall

SOURCEBOOKS, INC.
NAPERVILLE, ILLINOIS

Published by Sourcebooks, Inc.
P.O. Box 4410, Naperville, Illinois 60567-4410
(630) 961-3900
FAX: (630) 961-2168
ISBN 1-57071-630-7

Printed and bound in Thailand

IM 10 9 8 7 6 5 4 3 2 1

This book is dedicated to my angel

Katy

Acknowledgments

Special thanks to Ashland Christian School and Taft Elementary in Ashland, Ohio; and Eastview Elementary in Mansfield, Ohio, for helping me make my deadline! Thanks to all the amazing artists who sent beautiful illustrations I just couldn't fit into these pages. And thanks to all of you who talked to me about angels or wrote me your secrets. You're all angels!

Introduction

I traveled across the United States, visiting elementary schools and learning about angels from "the mouths of babes," our children. They freely passed along their insights and imaginations with enthusiasm, spirit...and a bit of humor. In addition to these interviews, I received hundreds of responses over the Internet and through the mail. Then, armed with the children's delightfully genuine thoughts about angels, I enlisted the help of hundreds of young artists—from the classroom to libraries to neighborhoods. I believe you'll be as amazed as I was at the creativity and talent at work in their illustrations. Enjoy!

Dandi Daley Mackall

What Children Know about Angels

What I don't get about angels is why, when someone is in love, they shoot arrows at them.

Sarah, 7

1

Heather Karkalik, 12

When angels talk to God, they always say "Hallelujah!" It means "Awesome!" - Benton, 9

Laura Prosser, 10

4

What Children Know about Angels

Some angels in heaven sleep standing up. Some stay awake all night because they are too close to the sun. I don't know about your angel, but mine sleeps with me.

Robert - 6

Michael Ruegen, 7

6

What Children Know about Angels

Angels deliver messages in different ways. Sometimes it's just a letter you get under your pillow, signed, "Love, God." Some of the lazier angels just throw the message down and make gravity do all the work.

Jason, 7

Kristin Smith, 9

What Children Know about Angels

I think an angel's life is like a sweet-smelling rose. During the day they watch over me and you, and at night they kiss our checks. That's where we get freckles from. They close their eyes to see if we have any bad dreams, and if we do, they take them away.

Mallory, 9

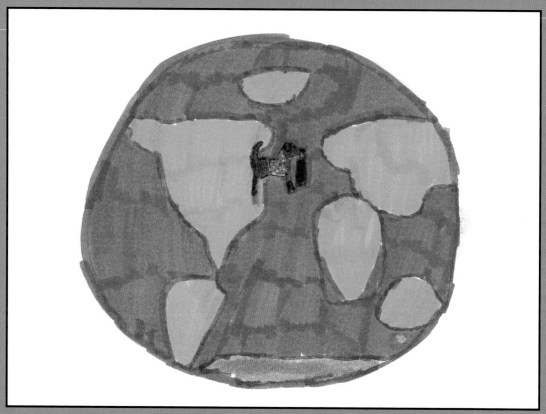

Keira Donelson, 11

What Children Know about Angels

Some of the angels are in charge of helping heal sick animals and pets. And if they don't make the animals get better, they help the kid get over it. —
                                    Vicki, 8

Michelle Crute, 12

What Children Know about Angels

Angels can fly because they have a very strong motor under that robe, and they know how to use those secret halos. — Justin, 8

Franz Konczak, 12

What Children Know about Angels

Angels talk Bible-talk, and when they do it sounds like an eagle flying. And they can talk in every language without even moving their lips.

Samantha, 9

Christina Rueger, 8

What Children Know about Angels

I'd like to be an angel and fly people to heaven just after they're dead and watch the look on their faces when they see God!

Katie, 10

Sheri Gonzalez, 13

What Children Know about Angels

Angels sing when you do something your mom tells you the first time.

Moms faint.

Opal, 8

Sheridan Hentrich, 7

What Children Know about Angels

After you live in heaven for a little while, other angels rub off on you in heaven. And before you know it, you're an angel.

Anthony 8

Kyle Wolff, 12

What Children Know about Angels

Sometimes they get a few bad angels in heaven by mistake. Then the devil sneaks into heaven when nobody's looking and steals the bad angels away. And in the morning, all the good angels wake up and say, "Good riddance to bad angels."—Melissa, 7

Andrew Banghart, 12

What Children Know about Angels

I might not make a good angel.
I'd probably want to be flying all
over all the time. And there's a lot
more to the angel business than that.

Aaron, 9

Bryce Edwards, 12

What Children Know about Angels

Angels look like whatever

They're standing in front
of because you can see
right through Them. So if
They stand in front of you,
They look just like you. —
Keisha, 9

Sandy Lowry, 11

What Children Know about Angels

God made angels so he wouldn't be lonely up there. And God also made the angels because earth people can be a little boring sometimes. —Maretta, 7

Brittany Lee, 12

What Children Know about Angels

If we would listen, angels would tell us to believe in God, and they'd tell us the secret of how to find our mommies when we get lost.

Brittany, 6

Jordan Conkle, 11

What Children Know about Angels

You'd be amazed how much angels look like birds. Their wings are made out of feathers of very good birds.

— Brianna, 6

Rebecca Hartwell, 11

What Children Know about Angels

There are ladders up to heaven with angels all over. If an angel can't fly right yet, the angel can grab onto the ladder.
— Tristin, 9

Danielle Rueger, 9

What Children Know about Angels

Some angels have pets. But they can only have pets if it's one of the animels that's got soul -- like dogs... and birds.

Crystal, 9

Ryan Lawhorn, 9

What Children Know about Angels

My angel is my grandma who died last year. She got a big head start on helping me while she was still down here on earth.

Katelyn, 9

Kelsey Ferencz, 8

40

Angels don't talk much, and they never use cuss words. But when you die, angels open heaven and shout "Come on in!"

Serina 7

David Shifflet, 11

What Children Know about Angels

All angels are girls because they gotta wear dresses and the boys didn't go for it. —

Antonia, 9

Ashley Johnson, 8½

What Children Know about Angels

Angels eat bread and wine.
(But nobody gets drunk or fat
in heaven.)

Caleb, 10

Donna Huvler, 11

What Children Know about Angels

If I look up real quick when I'm done praying, I can see an angel going out the window with my prayer. — Dennis, 7

Allison Sneeringer, 12

Angels just love
peanut butter and jelly!

Ben, 8

Hannah Edmiston, 8

What Children Know about Angels

Angles listen to god and play keep-away from the Devil.
Deanne, 7

Drew Anderson, 11

What Children Know about Angels

A lot of your Angels look like my Grandpa In his Old Scratchy Robe.

Meagan, 8

Jessica Ann Zellner, 8

What Children Know about Angels

When I need them
most, my angel give me
angel hugs!
Ethan 7

Riethie Hunt, 9

What Children Know about Angels

Halos are big rings — like bathtub rings, but on your head.

William, 6

Hailey Wetta, 6

If I were an angel, there would be no shouting-- except at ballgames. And even then, you'd have to cheer for both sides.

Sean, 8

Jenna Roth, 7

60

Angels smell just like we would if we got all the bad smells out. —

Wallace, 8

Gavin Speelman, 9

What Children Know about Angels

Guardian angels are the kind everybody gets one of. They guard you so you won't sneak out your window after your parents are asleep. Guard angels go by your name in heaven. So mine's name is Eric. – Eric, 8

Matthew Carr, 11

64

What Children Know about Angels

angels live in cloud houses
made by God and his son, who's
a very good carpenter.

Jared, 8

Ivaly Garcia, 9

What Children Know about Angels

I Like angels because they can sing as good as I can.

Ivaly, 9

Alex Lowery, 8½

What Children Know about Angels

My angel helped me be alive
during a huge car wreck
So did my seat belt.

brandon 8

Leigha Seamans, 10

What Children Know about Angels

You can see angels when you're a really little kid. Then you think it's not cool to see them when you get older, so they stop letting you. —

Shane, 7

Ryan Rush, 10

What Children Know about Angels

When robbers hurt people, God gets mad at them and sends angels and the cops after them.

Kaitlin, 7

Christina Wilfong, 11½

74

What Children Know about Angels

Whenever I'm bleeding, my angel is right there with invisible Band aids.

Jacob, 7

Nathanael Thomas, 10

What Children Know about Angels

Some times angels fly up and down, back and forth between earth and heaven. They listen in on us then fly back up and tell God on us that we cussed   Paul, 8

Alex Whitney, 12

What Children Know about Angels

Angels have a lot to do, and they keep very busy. If you loose a tooth, an angel comes in through your window and leaves money under your pillow. Then when it gets cold, angels go north for the winter.

Sara 6

Joseph James, 9

80

Angels need halos
to hold their
hair out of their
eyes on windy
days when they're
flying.   Austin, 6

Timothy Napier, 8

What Children Know about Angels

Angels look just like you and me --
except for the wing part. - Jenna,
9

Sarah Thomas, 11

What Children Know about Angels

When an angel gets mad, he takes a deep breath and counts to ten. And when he lets out his breath, somewhere there's a tornado. Regan 10

Rachel Bush, 11

What Children Know about Angels

The only Animal angel I know about is elephants. But there might be some others I don't know about yet. I'm only six.
Thomas 6

Cassie Solinger, 12

I heard an angel,
but everybody else
thought it was the wind.

Nate, 7

Rebecca Hartwell, 11

90

What Children Know about Angels

An angel that's **really** a dog is called a _Bark-Angel._ —

Mannie, 7

Megan Arnold, 9

What Children Know about Angels

Angels wear shiny nightgowns that puff out lik a parachute for soft landings. After a while, many of them wear glasses like mine so they can be farsighted and see earth people better.

Kayla, 8

Kristen Edmonds, 12

Angels have to wear halos.

How else can we tell the good ones from the bad ones? Hint: Bad angels don't wear halos.

Timothy, 7

Matthew Kinstle, 7

What Children Know about Angels

Of course we can't see angels. That's just the way it is when you're made of air. — Luis, 9

Allison Gross, 8

I can make an angel happy
if I make funny faces!-
Adelina, 7

Alyssa Westfall, 11

What Children Know about Angels

God's Angels are the
Workers in a great big
factory they work at,
called heaven.

Sandi, 9

Ally Utley, 9

What Children Know about Angels

Some people look at the twinkling and see stars. I look and see angels. —
Liand, 10

Sebastian Vittardi, 7

I'd like to be an angel so
I could go through walls.
Now it hurts too much.
— Kathryn, 6

Christina Wilfong, 11½

What Children Know about Angels

Angels talk all the way while they're flying you up to heaven. The basic message is where you went wrong before you got dead.

Daniel, 9

Danielle Olson, 10

I don't want to be an angel.
I'd rather stay down
here with my blankie.

Lionel, 5

Sheri Gonzalez, 13

What Children Know about Angels

Very far up in heaven in a
special place God made for them, the
angels make their homes. And they have
a Merry-Go-Round. It's off limits
to everybody but angels.

Dylan, 6

Zachary Freer, 10

What Children Know about Angels

I tried to touch an angel once, but I kept falling right through to the other side of her.

Dallas, 8

Timothy Napier. 8

114

What Children Know about Angels

Angels come in boy and girl because I've **heard** from both Kinds. **The** Long-hair angels are **girls**... although it's getting **harder** and harder to tell **them** apart. —

Jasper, 8

Brenna Vitou, 8

What Children Know about Angels

your angel wings are made of glass. That's why you have to be very careful when you hug an angel. No rough-housing.

Dylan, 8

#954,751

Kyle Elkins, 10

118

When an angel gives you the answer for math, but you think he's wrong, so you miss that one -- that makes him angry. — Spencer, 10

Alexandra Richard, 9

120

What Children Know about Angels

If I were an angel, I'd teach the whole world how to thank God for itself.

Mitchell, 7

Rebecca Hartwell, 11

What Children Know about Angels

If you tickle them angels,
they'll laugh their heads off.

Corey, 7

Curtis Cowan, 11

What Children Know about Angels

Guardian angels are the only ones who can keep you from being hit by trucks. I know that from expeience.

Jeffrey. 11

Jessica Konczak, 10

126

What Children Know about Angels

Sometimes when we close our eyes, angles take us to God to have a little talk.

Katie, 7

Franz Konczak, 12

What Children Know about Angels

If you want to make your angel very sad,
go ahead — talk to strangers or
forget Mother's Day. Your angel won't
be happy, and neither will you.

— Leo, 7

Sarah Rose, 10

What Children Know about Angels

Angels feel exactly like your foot feels when it falls asleep and gets tingly.

Wayne, 7

Emily Dohner, 8

What Children Know about Angels

I know a secret about how you get to be an angel. If you haven't always been an angel, you're never gonna be an angel in heaven. —Benjamin, 9

Kyle Wolff, 12

What Children Know about Angels

The only thing that gets in the way of an angel delivering its message is you. If you keep on talking yourself and don't listen, you'll never get it!

Teresa, 10

Olivia Wetta, 8

What Children Know about Angels

Here's a **secret** about angels: You better be nice to strangers. They could be secret angels. And if you're real bad, they can turn you into a frog. — Mariah, 8

Ryan Ramsey, 11

What Children Know about Angels

Angels make the world safe for kids. They keep us from getting too hurt. Usually it's one-on-one coverage. But with my brother, it takes about 100 of them to one of him." – Michael, 9

Amanda Laing. 7

What Children Know about Angels

I don't got an angel of my own because my mom, my sister, and me share one. I can't ever remember his name. But it's okay, He forgets my name, too.

Sean, 6

141

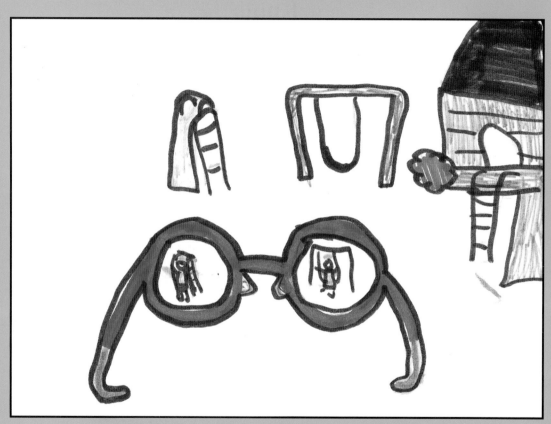

Rebecca Hartwell, 11

I can see angels because I wear glasses now. — Gregory, 6

Molly Brown, 13

What Children Know about Angels

Angels don't eat
but they drink
milk from holy cows.

Jack,
6

145

Suzana Clow, 6

I think I'd be a good angel. I'd be great at telling God what people are doing that they shouldn't be doing. My whole family say I'm a great tattle tale.

Chris, 7

Hailey Wetta, 6

What Children Know about Angels

Angels help me when I'm scared. And I get scared a lot. So that keeps a lot of them real busy.

James 5

Allison Beckman, 7

150

What Children Know about Angels

Angels guard and protect us from danger. I think every time we get hurt, an angel goes and thinks, "How could I let that happen?"

Kevin, 10

Amanda Laing, 7

152

You should always listen to messages angels bring you from heaven. I think if you don't listen to angel messages, they send messages to your mom telling on you And that's why mother's know everything.

Thomas, 6

Hannah Westfall, 8

What Children Know about Angels

If angels could talk, they would tell us Bible stories all the time. Then they would tell you why God made you, if you could stay awake for it.

Dawn, 7

Adam Sprang, 11

What Children Know about Angels

My guardian angel helps me with math, but he's not much good for science.

Henry, 8

Alyson Hout, 12

I was talking to God once, and I saw this angel, and we said,

"Now that's one nice looking angel!"

Willis, 10

Kasey Burson, 12

What Children Know about Angels

I never see angels. Angels only come down at night. And I always have to go to bed when all the good stuff happens. —Claire, 6

Tyler Whitmore, 9

What Children Know about Angels

Angels work for God and watch over kids when God has to go do something else.

Mitchell, 7

Amber Stevens, 12

164

What Children Know about Angels

I think angels smell a lot like clouds, but that's just me.

— Hermione, 9

Zachary Moysi, 13

166

What Children Know about Angels

It's not easy to become an angel! First, you die. Then you go to heaven. Then there's still the flight training to go through. And then you got to agree to wear those angel clothes. —Matthew, 9

Aaron Key. 9

What Children Know about Angels

I only know the names of two
angels. Hark and Harold Angels.
Gregory. 5

Rebecca Hartwell, 11

170

What Children Know about Angels

There are no animal angels... because animals never die. like if you have cats and they get old and one day you come from school and they're not there. they just wander off to see the world and you can't never find them again." - Becka, 6

Mariah Marshall, 8

Some angels
like to play
in the park
with kids.
We don't
mind. Art. 6

David Figley, 10

Angels know how to talk, but the trouble is that they only talk opera.

Benjamin, 8

Briana Burtin, 8

176

What Children Know about Angels

I hear angels all the time in my dreams.
And I'm sticking with that no matter how
many people tell me I'm crazy. — molly, 8

Erin Mahin, 7

I touch angels in my heart
when my mommy hugs me.
Julie, 6

John McNally, 9

What Children Know about Angels

I can't Believe everybody doesn't know what angels look like! Haven't you seen a ghost? They look like that.

Christopher, 9

Tori Sturnioli, 7

What Children Know about Angels

I know how many angels can fit on the head of a pin. One. But two can do it if they share. — Juan, 6

Peter Kim, 11

What Children Know about Angels

Crossing the street without permission will make your angel mad.

Irene, 7

Tricia Lykins, 9

What Children Know about Angels

This is a **secret** to grown-ups, but not a **secret to** kids. Angels come out and play **with** us kids at night when **grown-ups** are sleeping. – Dennis, 6

Debbie Lowry, 12

What Children Know about Angels

God made angels to protect us when it's dark and our moms all of a sudden decide we're to old for our blankies and nights lights. —Timothy, 7

John Collins, 11

What Children Know about Angels

EVERYBODY'S GOT IT ALL WRONG. ANGELS DON'T WEAR HALOS ANYMORE. I FORGET WHY BUT SCIENTISTS ARE WORKING ON IT.

OLIVE, 9

What Children Know about Angels

I heard an angel when I fell in the lake and almost drowned. At first it sounded like ~~glub, glub~~. Then I knew it was saying "Love, love."

Tess, 9

Artistic Angels

Attention Artists!

If you or your child would like to contribute to a future edition of
What Children Know about Angels,
please contact Dandi Daley Mackall at dmckall@ashland.edu.

Dandi Daley Mackall

is the author of more than 250 children's books and twenty-nine books for adults, including *God Made Nighttime Too*, the *Horsefeathers!* series, *God Made Me* (in its tenth printing), *Kids Say the Greatest Things About God*, and *101 Ways to Talk to God*. Her books have sold more than three million copies. She writes from rural Ohio, where she lives with her husband, her three children, two horses, a dog, and a cat.